Patterning Techniques

Doodling and patterning are wonderful ways to embellish your images to make them unique to you and really stand out! You can add doodles to a design before coloring or after. Adding doodles after coloring works best on designs colored with markers, as described below.

Tips

- Sketch your doodles in pencil first so you can erase mistakes if needed.
- Try colored pens, black pens, gel pens, or fine-tip markers to doodle your designs.

Before Coloring

1 Start with a blank design.

2 Add little doodles like lines, circles, and other shapes. Patterns are just simple shapes that are repeated!

3 Color the design.

After Coloring

1 After coloring a design with markers, add details using fine-tip pens.

2 Add more details using gel pens (I used glitter gel pens here).

3 Add a final layer of detail using paint pens.

Tips

- Try adding details with pens, gel pens, paint pens, fine-tip markers, colored pencils, and anything else you can think of!
- Try layering different media on top of one other to see what effects you can create.

Shading

Shading is a great way to add depth and sophistication to a drawing. Even layering just one color on top of another color can be enough to indicate shading. And of course, you can combine different media to create shading. Here are two techniques to try!

Shading by Outlining

If you've never tried shading before, start with this easy outlining technique to help make your images pop! In this example, markers were used for both the base colors and the outlines, but you could also create the outlines with pens, gel pens, or colored pencils.

Tips

- You can reverse the steps by outlining the design first and then coloring it in with lighter colors.

- Try putting the colors next to each other instead of on top of each other. For example, draw marker outlines, and then fill in the remaining open space with colored pencil.

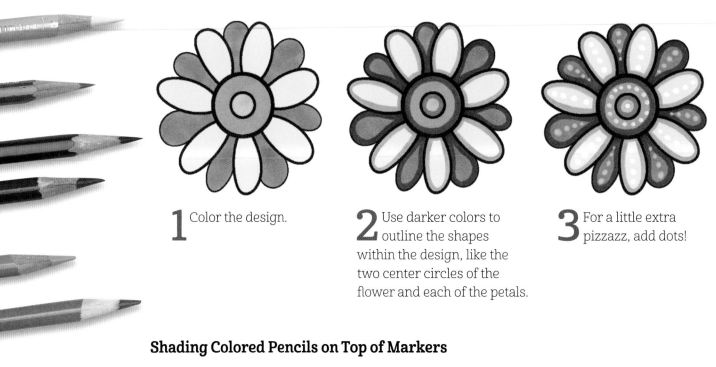

1 Color the design.

2 Use darker colors to outline the shapes within the design, like the two center circles of the flower and each of the petals.

3 For a little extra pizzazz, add dots!

Shading Colored Pencils on Top of Markers

1 Color your image with markers.

2 Use darker shades of your base colors in colored pencil to add shading. Here I used orange pencil to shade the yellow marker.

3 I used magenta and violet pencils to add shading to the pink marker areas.

Blending

Blending allows you to make smooth transitions between different tints and shades of a color when shading, and even between two different colors when creating gradients. Here are some simple techniques to produce flawless blends.

Alcohol-Based Markers

Alcohol-based markers can create smooth blends that have a painted look. You only need two colors to create a blend, but in this example I've used three shades of the same color: a light, a dark, and a color in between.

Tips

- It's easiest to create smooth transitions while your base layer is still damp.
- Don't be afraid to really work the marker into the paper—alcohol-based markers won't tear or pill the paper.
- Put a sheet or two of scrap paper underneath your coloring page to soak up any excess color that may seep through the paper.

 **1** Color your entire image with the lightest color. While this is still damp, use your middle color to add shading, focusing on the sides and bottom half of the shape.

 **2** Using your lightest color, go over the edges where the two colors meet to soften the transition.

 **3** Use your darkest color to add deeper shadows, focusing on the very outer edges and bottom of the shape.

 **4** Use your middle color to soften the edges between the dark and middle colors. If needed, use your light color on top of everything to smooth the transitions even more.

All of the colors in this flower were blended. Note the transitions from yellow to orange, from light pink to magenta, and from light blue to medium blue.

Tips

- When using colored pencils, apply more pressure to the areas that you want to appear darker.
- Use light-colored pencils on top of dark areas to create highlights.

4 I used a dark blue pencil to shade the light blue marker areas. You can also use a white pencil to add details on top of the marker, as I did in the flower's center.

Colored Pencils

In this example I've used three shades of each color:
a light, a dark, and a color in between.

1 Color the design with your lightest colors. Then, lightly apply your middle colors over the areas that you want to appear darker.

2 Lightly apply your dark colors where you want the deepest shadows. Apply more pressure where you want the color to be the strongest.

3 Use your middle colors to go over the area where the middle and dark colors overlap. Apply pressure as necessary to smooth the transitions.

4 Use your lightest colors to go over the areas where the light and middle colors overlap, applying pressure as needed.

Tips

- Applying a colored pencil in a circular motion makes the color appear more seamless than if you use back-and-forth strokes.
- Always use light pressure at first, and apply more pressure as you add more layers.
- A slightly blunt colored pencil works better for this technique than one with a super sharp point.

Colored Pencils with a Blender Pencil

1 Lightly apply color using small overlapping circles (as opposed to back-and-forth strokes). Leave areas completely white where you would like to create highlights.

2 Using the same colored pencil and the circular motion, go back and add a second layer of color, applying more pressure to the areas that you want to appear darker.

Colored Pencils with Baby Oil

1 Color the darkest areas first.

2 Next, color in the lighter areas.

3 Dip a cotton swab or tortillon (paper blending stump) into baby oil. Blot the excess on a paper towel. Gently rub the swab over the colored areas. Use a different swab for each color group. After the baby oil has dried, you can add more color if needed and use more baby oil to blend it.

Tips
- You can apply as many colors and layers as you like before applying the baby oil.
- A little baby oil goes a long way. It helps to pour a small amount into a watercolor palette or small container.

3 Go over everything with a blender pencil, using it the same way you would use a colored pencil. The blender will smooth your colored pencil marks and increase the intensity of the color.

4 You can create additional shading using a darker color, as I've done at the end of each petal. Repeat these steps with different colors for the rest of your design.

Tips
- Practice on scrap paper to see the various results you can produce by mixing different colors.
- After you apply the blender pencil, the surface of the art will be slick, so you might not be able to apply more colored pencil on top.

Color Theory

One of the most common questions beginners ask when they're getting ready to color is "What colors should I use?" The fun thing about coloring is that there is no such thing as right or wrong. You can use whatever colors you want, wherever you want! Coloring offers a lot of freedom, allowing you to explore a whole world of possibilities.

With that said, if you're looking for a little guidance, it is helpful to understand some basic color theory. Let's look at the nifty color wheel in the shape of a flower below. Each color is labeled with a P, S, or T, which stands for Primary, Secondary, and Tertiary.

Working toward the center of the six large primary and secondary color petals, you'll see three rows of lighter colors, which are called tints. A **tint** is a color plus white. Moving in from the tints, you'll see three rows of darker colors, which are called shades. A **shade** is a color plus black. The colors on the top half of the color wheel are considered **warm** colors (red, yellow, orange), and the colors on the bottom half of the color wheel are considered **cool** colors (green, blue, purple). Colors opposite one another on the color wheel are called **complementary**, and colors that are next to each other are called **analogous**.

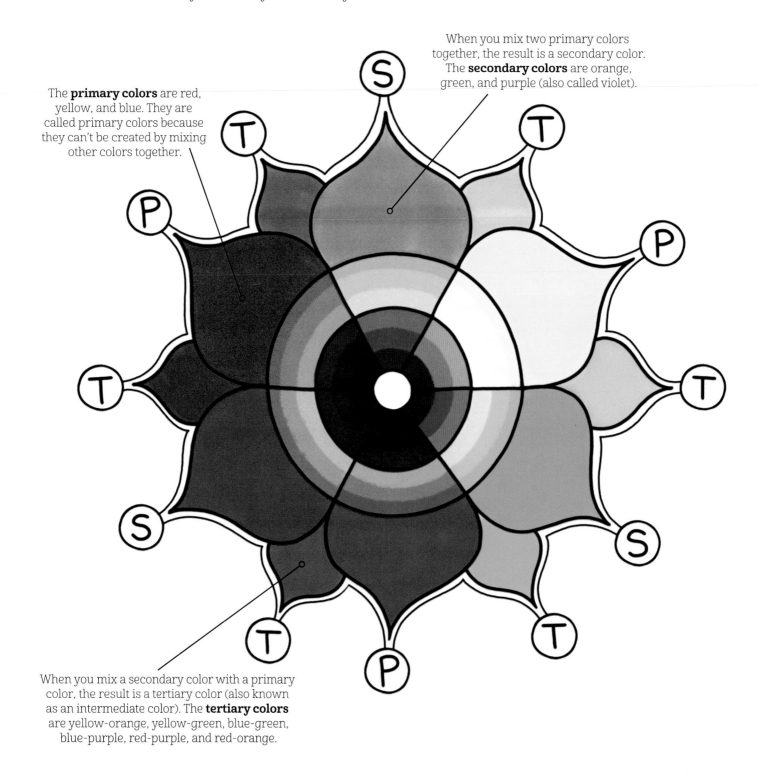

When you mix two primary colors together, the result is a secondary color. The **secondary colors** are orange, green, and purple (also called violet).

The **primary colors** are red, yellow, and blue. They are called primary colors because they can't be created by mixing other colors together.

When you mix a secondary color with a primary color, the result is a tertiary color (also known as an intermediate color). The **tertiary colors** are yellow-orange, yellow-green, blue-green, blue-purple, red-purple, and red-orange.

Color Combinations

There are so many ways to combine colors that sometimes it can be overwhelming to think of the possibilities...but it can also be a ton of fun deciding what color scheme you are going to use!

It's important to remember that there is no right or wrong way to color a piece of art, because everyone's tastes are different when it comes to color. Each of us naturally gravitates toward certain colors or color schemes, so over time, you'll learn which colors you tend to use the most (you might already have an idea!). Color theory can help you understand how colors relate to each other, and perhaps open your eyes to new color combos you might not have tried before!

Check out the butterflies below. They are colored in many different ways, using some of the color combinations mentioned in the color wheel section before. Note how each color combo affects the overall appearance and "feel" of the butterfly. As you look at these butterflies, ask yourself which ones you are most attracted to and why. Which color combinations feel more dynamic to you? Which ones pop out and grab you? Which ones seem to blend harmoniously? Do any combinations seem rather dull to you? By asking yourself these questions, you can gain an understanding of the color schemes you prefer.

Tip

Now you're ready to start experimenting on paper. When you're getting ready to color a piece of art, test various color combos on scrap paper or in a sketchbook to get a feel for the way the colors work together. When you color, remember to also use the white of the paper as a "color." Not every portion of the art piece has to be filled in with color. Often, leaving a bit of white here and there adds some wonderful variety to the image!

Warm colors

Cool colors

Warm colors with cool accents

Cool colors with warm accents

Tints and shades of red

Tints and shades of blue

Analogous colors

Complementary colors

Split complementary colors

It was only a sunny smile,
and little it cost in the giving,
but like morning light it scattered the night
and made the day worth living.

—F. Scott Fitzgerald

Everyone needs beauty as well as bread, places to play in and pray in, where nature may heal and cheer and give strength to body and soul alike.

—John Muir

Floral Owl

Never be afraid to sit awhile and think.

—Lorraine Hansberry, *A Raisin in the Sun*

Mandowla

Be present in all things and thankful for all things.

—Maya Angelou

A wise person knows there is
something to be learned from everyone.

—Unknown

_____
_____
_____
_____
_____
_____
_____
_____
_____
_____

Life is a journey,
and if you fall in love with the journey,
you will be in love forever.

—Peter Hagerty

Ready to Fly

My advice to you is not to inquire into why or whither,
but just enjoy your ice cream while it's on your plate.

—Thornton Wilder

Knowledge speaks, but wisdom listens.

—Jimi Hendrix

_____

_____

_____

_____

_____

_____

_____

_____

_____

Menowlgerie

Few color combinations pop as fiercely as the watermelon clash of complementary pink and light greens!

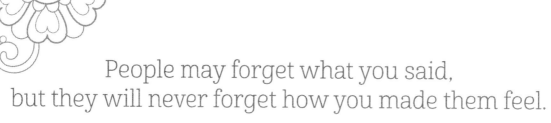

People may forget what you said,
but they will never forget how you made them feel.

—Carl W. Buehner

Lovey Owl

With careful attention to shading, you'll be able to make your leaves come alive in a dynamic frame for these night owls.

A good friend is like a four leaf clover:
hard to find and lucky to have.

—Irish proverb

_____
_____
_____
_____
_____
_____
_____
_____
_____
_____
_____

Crested Owls

Your first task should be deciding how to distinguish feathers from flowers. Hues farther apart from each other on the color wheel will make this easier!

Wherever you go, no matter what the weather,
always bring your own sunshine.

—Anthony J. D'Angelo

African Wood Owl

Sunbathing—this owl's breaking the rules! Think how you can follow suit with an unorthodox coloring scheme or pattern.

The sun's down and the moon's pretty—
it's time to ramble.

—Elvis Presley

Lesser Masked Owl

Make this owl's feather coat as busy as they come, but break the pattern by giving its big eyes a clean, two-tone look.

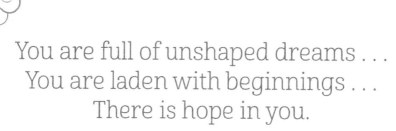

You are full of unshaped dreams . . .
You are laden with beginnings . . .
There is hope in you.

—Lola Ridge, "Wind in the Alleys"

Bright Eyes

Using a light-colored gel or paint pen, dab bright dots all over this owl's intense eyes—he'll look that much wilder!

To acquire knowledge, one must study;
but to acquire wisdom, one must observe.

—Marilyn vos Savant

Keeping Watch

Colored pencils and soft, candy-colored shades will give you
an owl that's so sweet you won't be able to look away!

What a wonderful life I've had!
I only wish I'd realized it sooner.

—Colette

_____
_____
_____
_____
_____
_____
_____
_____
_____
_____
_____

Beauty All Around

Thoroughly blended warm colors will give you a dreamsicle owl—soft and white on the inside and summery all over!

Realize deeply that the present moment
is all you ever have.

—Eckhart Tolle

_____
_____
_____
_____
_____
_____
_____
_____
_____

Cutie Pie

Style is a way to say who you are
without having to speak.

—Rachel Zoe

_____
_____
_____
_____
_____
_____
_____
_____
_____

The Well-Dressed Owl

The eyes have one language everywhere.

—George Herbert

_____
_____
_____
_____
_____
_____
_____
_____
_____
_____
_____

Here's Looking at You

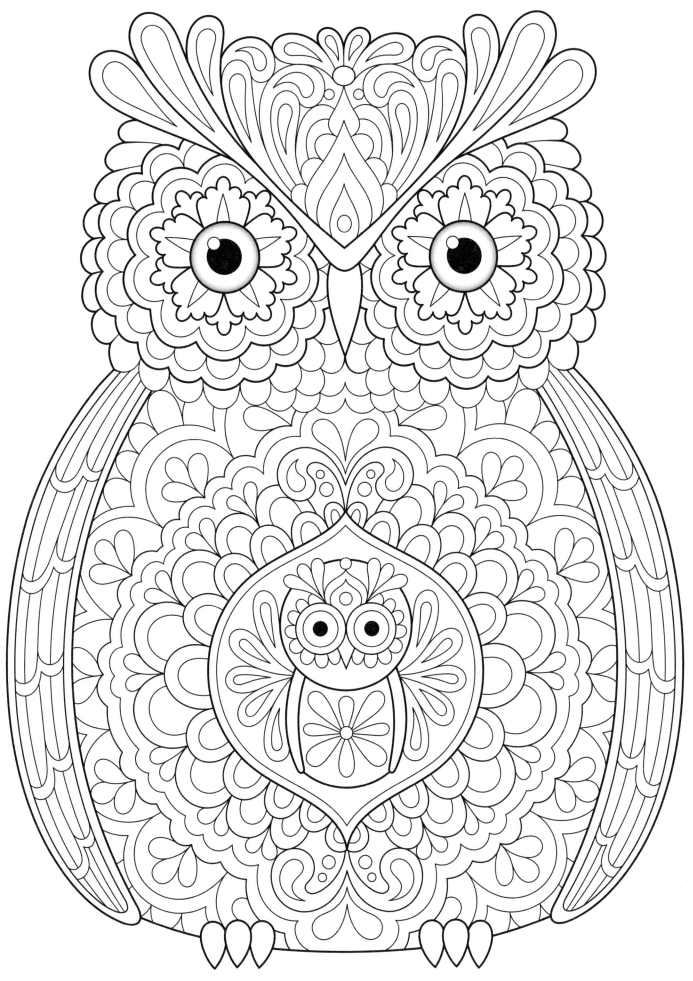

Love is that condition in which the happiness
of another person is essential to your own.

—Robert A. Heinlein

Togetherness

May the wind under your wings bear you
where the sun sails and the moon walks.

—J. R. R. Tolkien, *The Hobbit*

There's only one way to succeed in anything,
and that is to give it everything.

—Vince Lombardi

Determination

Happiness is a how, not a what.
A talent, not an object.

—Hermann Hesse

Owl Portrait

True friends are like diamonds—bright, beautiful,
valuable, and always in style.

—Nicole Richie

Owl Array

People will stare. Make it worth their while.

—Harry Winston

You can't go back and make a new start,
but you can start right now and
make a brand new ending.

—James R. Sherman

_____

_____

_____

_____

_____

_____

_____

_____

Gazing into the Future

Life is amazingly good when it's simple
and amazingly simple when it's good.

—Terri Guillemets

Greater Sooty Owl

Dreams are renewable. No matter what our age or condition, there are still untapped possibilities within us and new beauty waiting to be born.

—Dale E. Turner

Grey Owl

Tomorrow is always fresh, with no mistakes in it.

—Anne of Green Gables

Ever Hopeful

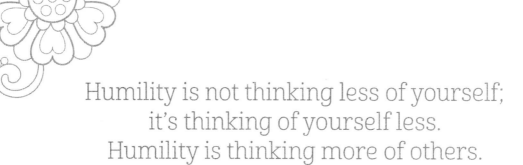

Humility is not thinking less of yourself;
it's thinking of yourself less.
Humility is thinking more of others.

—Rick Warren, *The Purpose Driven Life*

Why always "not yet"?
Do flowers in spring say "not yet"?

—Norman Douglas

Flower Power

You just get the vibes of your
surroundings and it rubs off on you.

—Gordon Lightfoot

Just Chillin'

The greatest pleasure in life is doing
what people say you cannot do.

—Walter Bagehot